Reality Strikes
True Stories About Kids

Bob Hugel

Laura D'Angelo

Denise Rinaldo

Christy Damio

Jonathan Blum

Emily Costello

John DiConsiglio

SCHOLASTIC INC.

New York Toronto London Auckland Sydney
Mexico City New Delhi Hong Kong Buenos Aires

4230500202744 2

Cover Photo
© Jason Tenaka Blaney

Contents

Introduction 4

Caught in Gambling's Grip: Lisa Hoffman
by Bob Hugel 6

Growing Up Multiracial: Daniel de la Cruz
by Laura D'Angelo 14

Surviving My Mom's Battle With Cancer
by Ralph Crespo as told to Denise Rinaldo 22

From Homeless to High School Graduate:
Zairia Benjamin
by Christy Damio 30

From Gang Member to Role Model
by Sergio Argueta as told to Laura D'Angelo . . . 36

Coming to the United States: Irene
by Jonathan Blum 44

Limited Vision, Unlimited Potential:
Isaac Goodpaster
by Christy Damio 49

Getting Himself Under Control:
De'Sean Harrison
by Emily Costello 56

Finding a Family: David Park
by John DiConsiglio 62

Introduction

Every kid has to deal with some tough stuff growing up. But the nine kids profiled in this collection have dealt with some of the toughest problems reality has to offer: addiction, discrimination, illness, violence, disability, and even death.

Their problems are varied. But all nine kids have one thing in common: They didn't let their problems keep them down forever. They found the help they needed to overcome their troubles and get their lives on track.

In this book, you'll find the story of Lisa. Her addiction to gambling cost her money, a job, and the trust of her family. But today, her debts are paid, and with the help of Gamblers Anonymous, she plans to stay away from casinos forever.

Then there's Sergio. As the leader of a violent gang, he seemed likely to wind up in jail—or dead. But after losing two good friends to gang battles, he realized that his life needed to change. Now, he runs a group that helps keep kids out of gangs.

Like Lisa and Sergio, the other kids in this book have faced difficult problems and come out on top. Daniel was ashamed of his ethnic heritage. Ralph's mother had a serious illness. Zairia spent two years in homeless shelters. Irene moved to a new country where she didn't speak the language.

Isaac has a serious vision problem. De'Sean is also dealing with a disability—as well as the death of both parents. David survived an abusive mother and several years in foster care.

Today, these young men and women are thriving. Several are in college, or headed there. Some have become role models, dedicating their time and energy to helping other troubled teens survive.

Think about these kids when reality strikes a blow in your life. Their stories show what it takes to turn a troubled life around.

Soon after she first entered a casino at age 18, Lisa became addicted to gambling. "Gambling took over my life," she recalls.

Caught in Gambling's Grip: Lisa Hoffman

by Bob Hugel

Lisa Hoffman of Moscow, Idaho, had long looked forward to turning 18. In her eyes and the world's, she would be an adult. Better still, she would finally be old enough to gamble legally in her state. "Growing up, I'd hear that I'd get to go to casinos or play bingo for money when I turned 18," Lisa recalls.

Lisa's mom and grandparents gambled. Her grandfather had once declared bankruptcy, in part because of gambling debts. Still, Lisa's family thought of gambling as an exciting and potentially profitable activity.

So, on the night of her eighteenth birthday, Lisa and her boyfriend, Rob, drove to the Nez Perce Indian reservation 30 miles from home. They strolled through the door of the Clearwater River Casino, into a plain room filled with video-game slot machines. Lights flashed.

Bells and buzzers sounded. Lisa felt like a winner.

When she left the casino that night, Lisa had lost only five dollars. But she brought home an urge to gamble that grew into an addiction. Within a year, she had gambled away several thousand dollars and lost her family's trust. "Gambling," Lisa admits, "took over my life."

Getting Hooked

Lisa isn't alone. Today, nearly two out of three teenagers gamble, according to the National Council on Problem Gambling, a nonprofit group based in Columbia, Maryland. That's a 17 percent increase from the early 1980s, estimates the council. Most teen gamblers play cards with friends, buy lottery tickets, or join Super Bowl pools. But about 1.1 million U.S. teenagers gamble compulsively, according to research by the National Academy of Sciences.

Compulsive gamblers are those who can't stop betting. To feed their habit, they may lie, cheat, steal, and neglect responsibilities. "It's vital that the public, especially teenagers, be made more aware that gambling can be harmful," says Dr. Durand F. Jacobs, clinical psychiatrist and spokesperson for the National Council on Problem Gambling.

At first, Lisa's gambling paid off. "Frequently, I'd go to the casino with $20 and walk out with $300 or $400," she says. "I didn't have a lot of money, and so it was a big thrill."

Lisa was in the early stage of a gambling problem. Compulsive gambling often begins with "a big win or wins," explains Laura Letson, executive director of the New York Council on Problem Gambling, a nonprofit group. "It feels so good, they keep gambling."

Lisa's winning stage lasted about four months. By then, she was spending all her free time at the casino. She'd go there alone and spend a few hours. Then she'd pick up her mom or a friend, and return to the casino, pretending she hadn't been there already. She entered what experts call the losing stage, and her losses began mounting. "I'd win a jackpot every now and then," Lisa says, "but everything I won went back into the slot machines."

Although Lisa worked part-time at a deli, she didn't earn enough to pay for her gambling habit. As she reached the desperation stage—the final step toward becoming a compulsive gambler—she began cashing bad checks.

Lisa also stole from her father. "I took hundreds of dollars at a time from his wallet," she says. "I'd rationalize that if I won money gambling, I'd pay the people I owed. But the money I won, I gambled away. Afterward, I'd sit in my car, cry, and beat my head against the steering wheel. I couldn't believe I had done it again. But by the next day, I'd tell myself it was my turn to win."

The bank sent letters home, and Lisa's father discovered her thefts. Confrontations became weekly events. Lisa would cry, apologize, and promise to stop gambling. But she couldn't. Her father hid his wallet. He and Lisa's mom hid and eventually burned Lisa's checkbook—but not until she'd racked up $1,400 in debts from bad checks. "My parents' friends told them to let me go to jail," Lisa says. "But they couldn't let me fall that far. They were hoping that I'd wake up, realize what I was doing, and get help."

In Gambling's Grip

Lisa's obsession began to make her physically ill—which is typical of compulsive gamblers. "I started getting migraine headaches," she says. In addition, Lisa sometimes arrived at the casino without clearly knowing how she had gotten there. She stopped caring how she looked and dressed.

"After a while, I didn't even care if I won or lost," she says, echoing a common attitude among compulsive gamblers. As Letson confirms, "At some point, it's not about winning anymore. It's about getting a fix from making a bet."

But even the act of betting was wearing thin for Lisa. "I hated to be there, but I could not stop going to the casino," she says. "It was the worst feeling. I felt so helpless."

In November 1997, a year after she fed her first dollar into a slot machine, Lisa was fired for stealing $120 from the deli where she worked. Two days before Christmas, her mother stepped in and begged the owner to give Lisa another chance. The woman agreed, but that night Lisa, who had a key, sneaked into the deli and stole $180 from the register. She lost it all in the slot machine.

Getting Help

Lisa had hit bottom. She had ruined her family's holiday and become a common thief. "It hit me, what I had done, and it made me sick inside," Lisa says. She knew she needed help. With her parents' support, Lisa went to a therapist, and then to Gamblers Anonymous.

To keep the bank from pressing charges, the Hoffmans covered their daughter's bad checks. They also covered her personal bills, credit card debts, and therapy costs—amounts that, Lisa estimates, totaled $10,000.

With the help of Gamblers Anonymous, Lisa

began understanding her problem. "Gambling is one of the most addictive things you can do, she says. "There are some people who can handle it, but I can't. I'll never be able to go to a casino again. The first time I do that, I'll be right back where I started."

A year after she quit gambling, Lisa was working as a home health aide and hoping to become a teacher someday. Looking back on her year as a gambler, she is still stunned by her actions, and she deeply regrets the pain she caused. "It was just one year of my life, but I completely destroyed everything I had worked for," Lisa says. "I have a very supportive and loving family, and I'll never have their complete trust again."

© Todd Bigelow

By the time he reached high school, Daniel was asking himself, "Where do I fit in? Should I learn more Spanish and hang with the Latinos? Or should I use the same slang as the black kids?"

Growing Up Multiracial: Daniel de la Cruz

by Laura D'Angelo

These days, when Daniel de la Cruz glances in the mirror, he sees a young man with a richly diverse ethnic heritage: Cuban, Mexican, Native American, and Irish. Yet, when others look at him, they simply see a young black man. Dealing with the difference between these two images hasn't always been easy for Daniel.

Left Out

Daniel was born in Los Angeles six minutes before his twin sister, Jessica. She has light olive skin, a freckled face, straight black hair, and closely resembles her Mexican father. Daniel has darker skin and looks like his mother, who is Cuban, Native American, and Irish. When Daniel and Jessica were growing up, strangers would often stare at them, unable to believe that the pair could possibly be twins.

"I used to tell Jessica she had it so easy," Daniel says. "In this society, she could go to an all-white country club and no one would look twice. I'd probably be asked to leave."

For Daniel's mother, this difference in the twins' appearance and the difficulty it caused was a chronic source of anxiety. "I felt sad knowing that this would become a lifelong issue between them," she says.

As Daniel grew older, he started asking himself: Where do I fit in? How should I dress? How should I act? Should I learn more Spanish and hang with the Latinos? Should I use the same slang as the black kids?

When Daniel enrolled at a Catholic boys' high school in Los Angeles, his choice seemed clear. "Since the population was mostly Latino, I felt pressure to be one of them. I felt I had to prove myself more because my skin was darker," he says. But Daniel's attempts to belong backfired painfully. The Latino students spoke far better Spanish than he did, and they mocked Daniel's struggles to speak the language. His inability to communicate left him

Daniel's heritage is Cuban, Mexican, Native American, and Irish. Here, he's surrounded by his family. From left to right are his sister, Jessica, his mom, Angela, and his brother, Gabriel.

outside their social circle.

Daniel was becoming more troubled and confused about his identity than ever. Eventually, he began to dread school. He cut classes and soon began skipping school altogether.

Daniel got the opportunity for a fresh start in tenth grade, at a public high school in Los Angeles. One day, a group of black girls were skipping rope and invited Daniel to join them. Later, some boys invited him to play basketball.

Daniel was heartened by their friendliness. "They seemed nice and I thought they'd be accepting," he remembers. He kept his Latino side concealed so his new friends wouldn't reject him. The school was predominately Mexican-American and black, and relations between the two groups were sometimes tense.

Faking It

More and more, Daniel's new friends included him in their activities. They even took him shopping for clothes, advising him on where to get the right sneakers, extra-wide-leg jeans, bright T-shirts, and a duffel bag. Daniel appreciated their efforts and jumped at the chance to belong. "I wished I was darker and could talk like the other guys to complete the image," he says.

The makeover didn't exactly turn out the way Daniel had expected. Pretty soon, Daniel's new clothes made him feel ashamed of himself. He realized that they were nothing more than a disguise, and he did not feel comfortable in them. "I thought, 'I can't believe the lengths I would go to just to be accepted,'" he says. "I felt like a fake."

Still desperate to fit in, Daniel felt pressured to conform to the crowd. Fearing rejection, he even betrayed his Latino roots by joining his friends when they made fun of the Mexican-American students. Then one day, he accidentally let a Spanish word slip out and knew instantly that his ruse was over. "I thought I had ruined everything," he says. "I felt like crying."

The rejection Daniel feared was not just paranoia; it was reality. A few weeks later, his new girlfriend abruptly dumped him. She called him a racist name for a Mexican, and the slur wounded him deeply.

After that, Daniel ate alone in the cafeteria. He questioned whether he would ever find acceptance: "I kept thinking about what had happened and what I could have done differently. Then I thought, 'I should embrace who I am. Just because I can't prove who I am to others doesn't mean I shouldn't be happy.'"

One day, a Mexican-American girl invited Daniel to sit with her and her friends during school. Daniel was grateful to be included but was also guarded. "I wanted to be accepted, but I didn't want to feel like I had to lie about myself," he says.

True to Himself

Finally, Daniel decided to reveal his secret. He told the Latino kids about his multiracial heritage. He explained that his lifelong dream was to visit Cuba, a country where people have a wide variety of skin colors. "Some are dark and some are light," Daniel says. "But there's not as much prejudice. People thought my dream was cool and that I was exotic."

By his senior year in high school, Daniel was splitting his time between twelfth grade and a city college. He was working hard academically and blossoming socially, but Daniel was getting some help. He credits a support group called Multiracial Americans of Southern California (MASC) with providing a place where he could feel accepted and comfortable with himself.

As a result of feeling better about himself, Daniel developed a much stronger relationship with his sister, Jessica. "We fight, but deep down, we're close," he says. Daniel now realizes that even though Jessica's appearance is different from his, she has shared his struggle to be accepted.

Daniel is anxious to help others who are still having a hard time. "It hasn't been easy for me," says Daniel. "I want to let other kids know what it took me a long time to figure out: Be proud of yourself and let people know who you are."

When Ralph was 12, his mom was diagnosed with breast cancer.
"I learned that talking about things can really help," he says.

Surviving My Mom's Battle With Cancer

by Ralph Crespo as told to Denise Rinaldo

My name's Ralph Crespo. In 1997, when I was twelve years old, my mom was diagnosed with breast cancer. The day I found out was one of the worst days of my life, and the years that followed were a terrible time for me.

But if I'd known then what I know now, things might have been a little bit better. If you're dealing with a similar situation, I hope my story will help you. And if you have a friend with a parent who's ill, maybe this story can help you help your friend. Here's what happened to me and my family.

As soon as I walked through the door that day, I knew something was wrong.

My mom was sitting on the couch in our living room, and she was totally still. She looked really sad.

"Mom, what's wrong?" I asked.

She didn't answer, so I asked again. "Mom, tell me!" Still, she stayed silent.

Worried, I went to my bedroom and closed the door. A while later, I peeked out through a crack in the door, and I saw that my mom was crying. My mother hardly ever cries, so I knew something serious was going on.

Later that day, she finally told me. "I have breast cancer," she said. "But it's nothing to worry about."

Family Crisis

Then my dad came home. He sat down and started talking to my mom. Then they hugged, and he started crying. That was the first time I'd ever seen my father cry. I was stunned.

I was just a kid when this happened and I didn't really know what cancer was. I thought it was a disease that kills everybody who gets it. I was terrified that my mom was going to die.

Shortly after she was diagnosed, my mom had surgery to have the cancer removed. My Aunt Natividad came from the Dominican

Republic to take care of me and my sister, Gisel, who was eight at the time. It felt weird coming home from school and not seeing my mom. Every time the phone rang, I was sure that it was bad news.

Tough Times at Home

When my mom came home about a week later, she still seemed really sick. I kept asking my aunt, "Is she going to pass away? What am I going to do?" She'd say, "She's not going to die, she's going to be here. Your mom is strong."

My little sister didn't know my mom had cancer. My parents had decided to keep it from her because they thought telling her would add more stress to the situation. But Gisel could tell something was wrong. She'd ask me, "What's wrong with Mom? Why is everybody crying?" I would get frustrated. I'd be like, "Gisel, leave it alone." But she'd ask again and again.

I think the whole thing made me closer to Gisel, though, because I had to protect her. I'd play house with her and do whatever she wanted to make her feel better. I knew that was what my mom wanted.

After my mom healed from the surgery, she started radiation treatments to kill any cancer that might be left in her body. The treatments made her really tired. Seeing her made me worry even more. I started just staying home with her.

It was summer, and I'd spend all day in her room. My mom would tell me to go out and enjoy myself, but I couldn't. My friends would come around and they'd ask, "What's up? Why don't you go out anymore?" I didn't want to talk about it, because every time I did, I'd start crying. They knew something was wrong with my mom, but that was it.

When school started in the fall, it was hard. I'd always had an 85 or 90 average, but that year I dropped down to 65 or 70—barely passing. And I did something that I really regret now: I quit playing football. My whole family used to go to games, and I knew it wouldn't be like that anymore. Also, I had this fear that my mom would pass away while I was playing a game, and I'd never get to say goodbye.

As my mom was finishing radiation treatments—and I saw that she still seemed pretty healthy—I started handling things better. I decided to find out more about my mom's cancer. So when I got a computer for Christmas, I researched breast cancer online. I was so relieved to discover that it's a disease that can be controlled and cured, especially in the early stages, and my mom luckily caught hers early.

Life Goes On

Then I joined a group at school called Sparks. It's a group in which kids help other kids. I felt more comfortable telling those kids what was going on. I learned that other people have problems, too, and that talking about things can really help. I even met one girl whose mom also had breast cancer, and now our moms are friends!

By eighth grade, my grades started improving and life was starting to feel normal. Still, my mom was depressed. She was afraid the cancer was going to come back. Then that

Ralph and his mom pose for a photo at home. If you have a sick parent, Ralph says, learn everything you can about the illness.

summer, we spent two months in the Dominican Republic. While we were there, the pressure just went away, and she got happy.

Now, four years after my mom first learned she had cancer, my family is doing great. At her latest checkup, she got a clean bill of health. Of course I'm not glad she got sick, but good things did come of it. My family is closer, and I've grown up a lot. My mom is more open-minded today. She tells me you only live once. She's going to tell me right from wrong and let me make my own decisions. Because of all I've been through, I try to do the right thing.

If anyone reading this has a parent who's sick, here's my advice: Learn about the illness. The more information you have, the better. Don't throw away activities you're involved with the way I threw away football. It's normal to feel low, but remember, your life isn't over. Don't lose hope.

© Lisa Marie Iaboni

Zairia and her family became homeless after they were evicted from this apartment building. "We had proof that my mom had paid the rent," Zairia states. "But they evicted us anyway."

From Homeless to High School Graduate: Zairia Benjamin

by Christy Damio

Imagine coming home and finding out that you'd been moved onto the street against your will. What would you do? Where would you go? In what ways would your life change?

Those are some of the questions Zairia Benjamin had to face when she was only 11 years old.

Eviction Notice

At age 11, Zairia had a pretty simple life. She lived with her mom and brother in Manhattan. She walked to school in the mornings with her friends. After school, she went to a program called "I Have a Dream." There, she ate snacks and got help with her homework.

But toward the end of fifth grade, Zairia's life changed forever. She and her mom came home and found an eviction notice on their door.

The notice said that Zairia's mom hadn't paid her rent. "We had proof that she'd paid, but they evicted us anyway," says Zairia. "The money-order pay stub was in the apartment, and we weren't allowed to go back in." With only a teddy bear and a few books, Zairia and her mother took a taxi to Zairia's grandmother's apartment, miles away in the Bronx.

Zairia's grandmother welcomed them. But her apartment was too small for Zairia, her mother, and her brother all to move in. Zairia, her brother, and her mom were homeless. They went to stay in the shelter system's Emergency Assistance Unit (EAU).

"It was horrible," Zairia says. "There was a whole bunch of families sleeping on the floor. They gave us a big plastic bag full of blankets and sheets. My mother didn't sleep. She just watched us sleep, because people would steal your things."

It was a scary situation, too—upsetting in every way. While Zairia's brother was asleep in the EAU, a centipede bit him on the eye. "It swelled really badly," Zairia says. "We had to rush him to the hospital."

The family moved around for two years in the shelter system. Finally, they got their own apartment. By the end of eighth grade, Zairia had a home in the Bronx.

Pursuing Her Dreams

Even though Zairia had a home, her life still wasn't easy. In tenth grade, she attended the neighborhood high school. It was a tough year for Zairia.

"You had to be at school at least 30 minutes ahead of time just to get into the building," she remembers. "The line to go through the metal detectors was outside. Rain, sleet, or snow, you were waiting outside to go through a metal detector."

Zairia did poorly that year. "I cut school a lot," she admits. "I went to my three favorite classes, but I never went to any of the other eight classes that I took. I failed the other eight."

By eleventh grade, Zairia had moved in with her grandmother and switched schools. The

Zairia was determined to go to college. Through a program called "I Have a Dream," she got help filling out college applications.

change of environment helped her focus on her studies.

Under her grandmother's supervision, Zairia attended night school to make up the credits she'd lost. She left regular school at 3:00. She went to night school from 5:00 until 9:00. When she got home around 10:30, she had to do her homework from regular school.

"The days that I didn't have to go to night school, I was working at Wendy's," she says.

"It was a really hectic year. But I passed all my classes, and I became a senior."

By that time, Zairia had a new goal. "Many people in my family didn't even finish the tenth grade," she says. "They dropped out. Once I got to the eleventh grade, I thought, 'I'm doing all this work. I might as well try to go to college.'" Soon, Zairia was back at the "I Have a Dream" program, getting help with college applications.

As she made plans to study liberal arts in college, it was hard to imagine that only a few years earlier, Zairia was sleeping on the floor of a shelter, with no idea where she'd end up. And even more recently than that, she was failing most of her classes. Zairia has been through tough times. But these days, she has a lot to look forward to.

© Jason Tenaka Blaney

As a teenager, Sergio belonged to a gang. Now he runs a group that helps kids stay in school and get out of gangs. "I still get angry, but I don't solve problems with my fists," Sergio says.

From Gang Member to Role Model

by Sergio Argueta as told to Laura D'Angelo

The first time I was arrested, the cop said to me, "Get used to the feel of these handcuffs—you'll be in them for the rest of your life." I was 13 years old. In the end, I proved that cop wrong.

I grew up in a low-income housing complex in Hempstead, Long Island, where the grassy suburbs of New York City turn into cracked concrete. My mother had moved to America to escape the war in El Salvador. At 5:00 A.M., she'd get up to scrub floors in rich people's houses in hope of giving me a better life.

I loved school when I was little and got along with both blacks and Latinos. But in middle school, being good was not the cool thing. Blacks and Latinos hated each other. One tradition was "Puerto Rican Day," when the black kids would get together and beat up the Latino kids. It didn't matter that we were El

Salvadoran or Nicaraguan. To them, we were all "Puerto Ricans."

Around that time, these older guys who had done jail time came back to our neighborhood. They greeted each other with choreographed handshakes. They were members of the Latin Kings gang. My friends and I idolized them. We started calling ourselves R.P., or Redondel Pride, after the nickname for our housing complex. Our colors were red, white, and brown. We didn't think of ourselves as a real gang, but if you jumped me with two of your boys, I'd catch you with five of mine. We went from fist fighting to mugging kids at the mall for their beepers and money.

Violence and Death

My best friend, Indu, was the only person I trusted outside of Redondel Pride. He refused to join our group because he was working hard to graduate from high school.

I got kicked out of school at the end of my freshman year, after I fought with a kid in the hallway. My mother was heartbroken that I was expelled. She fell to her knees, crying. She swore I'd never amount to anything. That hurt me and pushed me closer to my R.P. brothers.

At 16, I became the head of R.P. Our membership was 80 deep by then. The youngest member was 13, and the oldest was 28. I was going to a different school by then, and when I walked down the street, groups of kids would part to let me by.

I thought I had power, but I was powerless. One day five dudes from another gang started messing with my friend Indu. A fight broke out. Someone yelled in Spanish, "Take out the gun!" A bullet ripped through the back of Indu's head and killed him.

I was devastated. I watched his mother sob during the funeral and beg him to "wake up!" There was nothing I could do to stop the tears from pouring down my face. My pain turned to anger. I was going to make someone else feel that pain.

I hung low for a year, then my friend Ricky and I bought a shotgun and hid it in the trunk of his car. We planned to meet the next day to plot our revenge, but that night, outside of a dance club, Ricky and our friend J.C. ran into the gang that killed Indu. They clashed with their knuckles. Then Ricky grabbed the shotgun from the car. He pumped three times into the crowd. One man died that night. It was J.C. Ricky was arrested for the shooting.

I was crushed and confused. I had one brother lying in a coffin and another hiding his face on the TV news. But who was to blame? If I hadn't bought that gun, J.C. would still be alive.

My conscience ate away at me. I stopped calling meetings of Redondel Pride. I graduated from high school, but my life was heading nowhere. I didn't know anybody from my neighborhood who went to college, but I figured it had to be a way out. I enrolled in Nassau Community College and studied criminal justice. I knew something about the subject, having been arrested three times. I loved my classes and made the Dean's List.

I became president of the school's Latino organization, and we raised money to start scholarships. The next year, I was elected student-body president. I represented 23,000 students and helped oversee a $2.3 million budget. When I was accepted to Columbia University, an Ivy League school that attracts the top minds in our country, I couldn't believe it! Things were looking up for me.

But around me, things were falling apart. On a train ride home from the National Puerto Rican Day Parade in New York City, I hung out with this guy Eric. We got off the Long Island Rail Road at the Hempstead stop, and as we parted ways, Eric yelled, "Be safe!" Imagine my surprise when I learned the next day that members of a gang had beaten him to death because he was carrying a Puerto Rican flag.

The True Meaning of Power

That's when I realized that I couldn't just wait for politicians to do something. This is my community. Many kids who are now in gangs had once looked up to my friends and me. We blew our chance to guide them in the right direction. I wanted another chance. So I started

Sergio visits the grave of his best friend, Indu, who was killed by gang members. When another friend was killed trying to get even for Indu, Sergio realized it was time to change his life.

© Jason Tenaka Blaney

a service group called Struggling to Reunite Our New Generation, or S.T.R.O.N.G. Our logo is two hands prying open bars. A light shines through the opening, and there's a picture of a book with the words "Success" and "Education."

As the leader of S.T.R.O.N.G., I go to junior and senior high schools and tell my story to packed auditoriums. We work with law enforcement to create anti-gang workshops for kids. I'm finishing my degree at Hofstra University in Hempstead because after the first semester I couldn't afford the tuition at Columbia.

I still get angry, but these days, I don't settle problems with my fists. Every time I help a kid stay in school or get out of a gang, I feel the true meaning of power.

Irene and her family moved from Mexico to the United States. At first, Irene recalls, "I felt like I was in a different world. I was lost."

Coming to the United States: Irene

by Jonathan Blum

Irene, 18, was born in Puebla, Mexico. "I have good memories of my childhood," she says.

"I had cousins to play with," Irene recalls. She also had her mother, grandmother, and younger sister. But her father lived in Los Angeles. It was far away.

Irene's parents wanted a good education for their girls, but school expenses in Mexico were higher than the family could afford, so Irene's family moved to Los Angeles when she was nine.

Irene will never forget how hard it was. She had to say goodbye to her grandmother. "I remember it as clearly as if it were two days ago," Irene says. "She waved goodbye. It was so hard to look back and see her."

Irene was happy to see her father in Los

Angeles, but living there was a big change. In Mexico, there had been lots of open space. There were no freeways or streetlights there. Now Irene was in a huge, crowded city. "I felt like I was in a different world," she says. "I was lost."

Irene entered fifth grade. She could only speak a few English words. She got two F's and a D on her first report card. Her father was upset. "He told me, 'I'm not sending you to school to get this type of grade,'" Irene remembers. "After that, I made it my goal to get straight A's."

Mastering English

Irene was doing better by ninth grade. She became more confident in her English. "Before, I couldn't even stand being in class. I would blush. I would feel my head boiling," she recalls. "As time passed, I learned to speak in front of a class. I learned how to have a conversation."

Irene also started volunteering. She joined groups. She followed her interests in medicine, business, graphic arts, and public speaking.

Then Irene joined a program called OnRamp Arts. Through the program, she began writing and designing online games.

In the games, players go on quests. They try to reach goals. Irene and her classmates sometimes based the quests on personal experiences. They also used their imaginations and Latin American history.

Irene and her group designed a game called *Making of the Delicious Tamale*. The game follows the adventures of a young Latina named Leecha. She explores her roots to find out how to make a tamale—a Mexican treat that's made with cornmeal.

Irene says the creative projects that teens have accomplished at OnRamp show what they can do. It helps break stereotypes about Latino teens in L.A.

"We are showing that we are capable of doing this. Give us a chance," she says. "OnRamp Arts gives us the opportunity to create our own stories."

Irene's next big challenge was affording

college. She planned to study business and graphic arts. She knew it would be expensive. But she was determined to do everything in her power to make it happen.

Irene has some advice for other kids who have moved to the United States from different countries. "If you're an immigrant, a lot of things get in your way," Irene says. "Always look at them not as obstacles, but as challenges."

Limited Vision, Unlimited Potential: Isaac Goodpaster

by Christy Damio

When Isaac Goodpaster was a kid in Kentucky, he was a good athlete and student, but he never did well at reading and writing. "Those were always my two hardest subjects," he remembers.

When he got to middle school, Isaac had even more trouble reading. The print was smaller in his schoolbooks. Reading small print gave Isaac headaches. One day, the school gave eye tests to the students. "They were like, 'You need to go see a doctor,'" remembers Isaac. "It wasn't until then that I knew I had bad vision."

Isaac soon learned that his vision was *very* bad. Perfect vision is 20/20. That means that from 20 feet away, you can see what any perfectly sighted person would see from 20 feet away. Isaac's vision was 20/200. That means that when he stood 20 feet away from

His vision is seriously impaired. But that has not stopped Isaac, a gifted athlete, from excelling at football and other sports.

something, he could only see it as well as a person with perfect vision would see it from 200 feet away.

The doctors tested Isaac's eyes, looking for what was wrong. The tests were painful. "They put my head in a machine and shined an intense light into a metal instrument on my eyeball," says Isaac. "With that bright light shining, they probed my eye."

Finally, the doctors told Isaac that he had a condition called Stargardt's disease. Isaac's condition has no cure. Glasses would do very little to help Isaac.

A Different World

Before he was diagnosed, Isaac thought everyone's vision was just like his. But his was very different from most people's. Isaac's central vision—the way he sees things that are right in front of him—was much more blurry than his peripheral vision—or the way he sees things from the top, bottom, and corners of his eyes. Things were hardest to see if he looked directly at them. "If I really want to see someone, I might look above them," he says. "If I'm staring at somebody eye to eye, I cannot see their eyes."

Adjusting to Change

Isaac's school wanted to help him. They provided him with a machine used for reading. It had a screen that enlarged the print in his books. But using the machine was embarrassing. "They wanted me to wheel this huge thing around middle school. I was like, 'Yeah, right. You just leave that in this room. If I need it, I'll come and get it,'" Isaac recalls.

Isaac also began using books with large print, books on tape, and other new ways of learning. When other students saw Isaac learning differently, some teased him. Isaac remembers feeling embarrassed. "It was terrible," he says.

It took Isaac a while to adjust to the changes in his life. But when he decided to accept the way things were, he started to feel better. "After the first two years, I finally realized that it didn't matter what the other kids thought, because I

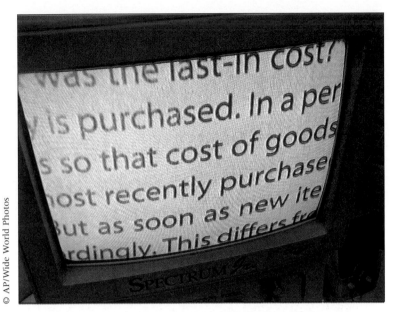

was the last-in cost?
is purchased. In a per
so that cost of goods
ost recently purchase
But as soon as new ite
rdingly. This differs fr

SPECTRUM

Isaac uses a machine like this to help him read. The machine makes small type appear bigger, so Isaac is able to read it.

was happy with my life," he says.

After he got used to new methods of learning, Isaac was much more comfortable. He'd always been good at sports, so he focused on being an athlete. Even with his bad vision, he was agile enough to excel at any sport he played. He won many honors in high school football, and he broke the Montgomery County career receiving record in his junior year.

Using his peripheral vision and his memory,

© AP/Wide World Photos

Isaac was recruited to play football at Wofford College in South Carolina. In his junior year, he was the team's leading receiver.

he got so good at football that Wofford College in South Carolina recruited him to play on its team. They gave him a full scholarship. In his junior year at Wofford, Isaac was the school's leading receiver with 25 catches for 422 yards and two touchdowns.

By the time he reached his senior year at Wofford, Isaac had developed a number of strategies for handling his schoolwork. These days, he always sits in the front of the classroom. Sometimes he can see what's written on the board, sometimes he can't. Either way, it's okay. Isaac learns best by listening. "My reading comprehension is terrible," he says, "but my listening comprehension is really good. So when professors are giving lectures, I can take notes from just listening to what they're saying."

Isaac doesn't get headaches from reading anymore. Large print, special computer equipment, and books on tape have changed that forever. Because he was willing to try new things, Isaac's life got much easier. Now he's a success in school. And, most important of all, he's happy.

Though he struggles with ADHD, De'Sean has reason to smile. Since he discovered writing, he's written dozens of poems.

Getting Himself Under Control: De'Sean Harrison

by Emily Costello

As De'Sean Harrison, age 17, makes his way through the sunny lunchroom at Marblehead High School, friends call out to him. "Hey, De'Sean!" they say.

De'Sean gives one a shy smile and another a high five. For the most part, he enjoys high school life in Marblehead, Massachusetts. But he has faced some major challenges during his teen years.

De'Sean has a learning disorder called Attention Deficit/Hyperactivity Disorder (ADHD). As many as seven out of a hundred American kids are born with this disorder. Kids with ADHD struggle to pay attention in class. They fight to control their emotions. About half drop out of school.

De'Sean has an angry streak. And when other students upset him, he doesn't always manage to keep his cool. He is sometimes sent home for yelling at classmates or pushing them.

Still, unlike many kids with ADHD, De'Sean likes school. His teachers help him to stay focused and control his temper. Things were going well until the winter that his mother got sick.

Fatally Ill

De'Sean's mom became ill with pneumonia, an infection of the lungs. She had caught it once before. It had almost killed her, and it had left her lungs dangerously weak.

So De'Sean was relieved when the doctors released his mom after a few days in the hospital. He expected her to get better at home.

Instead, his mom became much sicker. De'Sean's aunt rushed her back to the hospital. But it was too late. She died a few hours later.

"I miss her wonderful smile," De'Sean says. Losing his mom was especially hard because his father had died when De'Sean was in the sixth grade. "I thought the world was over when my dad died," De'Sean remembers. His mother had helped him find the strength to go on.

Now, with both of his parents gone, De'Sean had to pack up his belongings and move to his Aunt Robyn's home.

At his aunt's house, De'Sean misses seeing family members who live in his old neighborhood. He misses his dog, Star. But the hardest part of living with his Aunt Robyn is getting to school.

De'Sean's aunt lives farther from Marblehead High School than his mom did. His uncle often drives him there in the morning and picks him up in the afternoon. De'Sean spends about an hour and a half on the road every day.

Maybe that's why he hasn't wasted much time feeling sorry for himself. The week after his mom died, De'Sean organized a can drive at school. The drive was in honor of a family friend who died of the blood disease leukemia.

De'Sean hung signs in all the hallways. Kids donated cans. De'Sean cashed in the cans. He sent the money to the hospital to use for

De'Sean enjoys English class. His teacher, Mrs. Dawes (far right) encourages him to express himself through writing.

leukemia research. "I can still help others," he told a teacher at the time.

De'Sean has found another way of dealing with his sadness. Last spring, Mrs. Dawes, his English teacher, asked him to write a poem. De'Sean did the assignment. But he didn't stop there. He kept writing.

De'Sean wrote poems about each of his teachers. He wrote about his friends and about his country. Now he keeps a slim notebook just for poems. He hopes to be a famous writer someday. "My poetry makes me proud," De'Sean says.

When he's sad, De'Sean tries to think about happy times. He remembers being the ring bearer at his mother's wedding. "She was the most beautiful person I ever saw on that day," De'Sean says.

Memories like that inspire De'Sean to work hard in school. "I want to finish high school," he says. "It's what my parents would have wanted."

David was removed from his mother's home when he was 11. He then spent four years bouncing from one foster home to another.

Finding a Family: David Park

by John DiConsiglio

David Park likes to talk about almost anything. Ask him about his studies at Radford University in Virginia, and David, 21, will excitedly explain every class. He can talk for hours about his grandparents, his plans to become a police officer, his girlfriend, Phyllis, music, and Duke basketball.

Just don't ask David about his past. When the subject comes up, he gets quiet. His naturally animated voice grows flat. He looks down at his hands and says, "I'm not proud of my past. I'd kind of like it to disappear."

Much of it already has. David hasn't seen his father since he was five. He last saw his mom at age 13. And what few memories he has of his parents, he'd just as soon forget. David grew up around drugs, drinking, and violence. "It wasn't what you'd call a happy childhood," he says.

When David was 11, he was taken out of his mother's home and placed in the foster-care system—the government program that takes care of kids who have no other place to go. David's long journey through foster care took him to three locked-down detention centers, two group homes and half a dozen foster families—all before he'd spent even one year in high school.

"I just wanted to be a normal kid and have a family like everybody else," David says. "But for me, that took a little longer."

Foster Care Nation

On any given day, half a million American kids are in foster care. Like David, most of them come from severely troubled homes, their lives shattered by neglect or abuse.

The foster system is meant to keep kids safe and secure. But, experts agree, the system is in shambles—understaffed and underfunded. There aren't enough qualified foster parents for all the kids who need them. And there aren't enough social workers to monitor foster families.

As a result, many kids get shuffled from home to home. According to a 2004 report, half of all children in foster care spend at least two years there, and can expect to live in at least three different homes. At 18, teens "age out" of the system, and often end up living on their own. These kids are more likely to drop out of high school, be unemployed, and have trouble with the law, the report says.

"Sometimes, foster kids are treated like they did something wrong," says Karen Jorgenson of the National Foster Parent Association. "But they are the victims. They are looking for help."

In Search of a Family

David's story begins in Los Angeles, where his parents moved from Seoul, South Korea. David was just a toddler then, but he remembers his father hitting his mother in an alcoholic rage. When David was five, his mother fled with him to Arlington, Virginia.

But life wasn't much better on the East Coast. David lived in a cramped apartment with his mother, grandmother, and little brother. His mother worked long hours as a waitress. She slept though much of the day, and drank through much of the night. "When I think of my mother, I think of the memories I don't have," David says. "Like family dinners, or her helping me with my homework. None of that ever happened."

Alcohol made his mom depressed and violent. David took the brunt of her beatings. His grandmother often hit him, too. Before he was 10, David ran away several times. He'd walk around downtown Arlington until he got cold. Then, with nowhere else to go, he'd sneak back into the house when everyone else was asleep.

At age 11, David's life changed for good. One day, while his mother was at work, David got into a fight with his grandmother. Running through the kitchen, he accidentally knocked over a bottle. His grandmother flew into a rage and beat him. Then she called the police—and reported that David was beating her.

"I didn't understand what was going on," David says. "I was 11 and the police were taking me away."

David's grandmother filed charges and 11-year-old David was taken to a juvenile detention center. For two months, he was locked in a unit with older kids, some of whom were already hardened criminals. David remembers his 16-year-old roommate scaring him with stories of robbing old women at gunpoint. Each morning David woke to the sounds of birds chirping in the courtyard and convinced himself that it had all been a dream. "Then I'd see those iron bars on the windows," he says, "and I'd know it was really happening."

Christmas came and went without a visit from his mom. Finally, David was transferred to a foster group home with other troubled youths. Frightened and confused, David was hard to handle. He cursed at the staff and refused to follow the house rules. "I was like a bottle of soda that had been shaken up for years," he says. "When you take the top off, it explodes."

For the next two years, David was shuttled between locked-down facilities and group homes. His mother visited him just a handful of times. But David still expected each stop to be his last. Eventually, he told himself, he'd be allowed to go home. "No matter how bad your family is," David says, "you always think about going back to them."

Those dreams were dashed when David was 14. At the time, he was living in a group home in Lynchburg, Virginia. His behavior had improved. He'd made friends and had even taken weekend outings with a social worker to play basketball and video games. His grandmother's charges against him had long since been dismissed.

But David hadn't seen his mother in months, and he wondered why it had been so long. His social worker finally told him: David's mother had left town. No one knew where she'd gone.

"It was my mother's way of telling me, 'I don't want anything to do with you. I'm moving on with my life—you move on with yours,'" David says. "That's when I gave up the idea of having a family."

No Place to Call Home

At 14, David was sent to live with his first foster family. For the first time in over two years, he went to school. But soon, David's new family decided to leave the foster system. For the next year, David bounced from temporary home to temporary home. At school, no one suspected that the cheerful teen who starred on the football and basketball teams went home each day wondering whether it was time to pack his bags.

In each new home, David felt like an outsider. Some of his foster families would take vacations and leave him behind. Others threw birthday parties for their own kids and never invited David. It had been years since anyone remembered his birthday. "You start thinking there must be something wrong with you because no one wants to take care of you," he recalls.

Then, when David was 15, he was sent to live with Steve and Patty Cook in Roanoke, Virginia. The Cooks were an older couple. They already had three grandchildren. They seemed

At 15, David finally found a permanent home with his loving foster grandparents, Patty and Steve Cook. Here, David relaxes with the Cooks on the porch of their home in Roanoke, Virginia.

nice enough, but David wasn't expecting much. He was sure it was only a matter of time before the Cooks got rid of him, too.

But David was wrong. Immediately, the Cooks told him that he could be part of their family. And, little by little, David started to believe them. "They kept telling me they loved me and cared about me. They treated me like their other grandkids," he says.

For the first time since he entered the foster care system at 11, David found presents under the Christmas tree with his name on them. And no family vacation was complete unless David came along. At a family party, Steve Cook introduced David as his grandchild. "I thought I was going to cry," David says. "I was 15 and, for the first time, I really had a family."

These days, David has no time to dwell on his past. He takes a full course load at Radford and works 40 hours a week as a security guard at an upscale spa.

Besides, David would rather look forward. "Five years ago, I never thought my future would look so good," he says. "That's one thing about foster kids. We have no place to go but up."